Tea Cup Tales

The Art of Reading Tea Leaves

Also by the author:

Poems That Tell Me Who I Am
Autumn Leaves
The San Diego County Writers and Publishers Resource Guide

The Art of Reading Tea Leaves

by Margaret Lange McWhorter

Ransom Hill Press

Printed in the United States of America
Book design and layout by Artichoke Editing & Print Design
Cover design and layout by Summer Andrecht

Ransom Hill Press
P. O. Box 325
Ramona, CA 92065

Publisher's Cataloging-in-Publication
(Provided by Quality Books, Inc.)

McWhorter, Margaret Lange.
Tea cup tales : the art of reading tea leaves / by Margaret Lange McWhorter ; illustrations by Summer Andrecht. – 2nd ed., rev. and updated.
p. cm.
Includes expanded dictionary of tea leaf images.
Includes bibliographical references and index.
ISBN: 0-941903-23-0

1. Fortune-telling by tea leaves. I. Title.

BF1881.M39 1998 133.3'244
QBI97-40572

To the child in all of us.

Acknowledgments

Thanks to my patient family who let me practice on them, especially my husband James, who now drinks tea in the morning instead of coffee and has learned to like it better. My daughter, Venus Andrecht, kept me at this book until I finished it.

Also, thanks to the many interesting people whose cups have made this book possible. Thanks to Elyse Kuhn, fellow tea leaf reader, who, without even reading the text, studied and read the teacup illustrations herein and came up with results that were stunningly similar to my own. That makes tea leaf reading almost a science, doesn't it? Many thanks also go to Donna Zick, who contributed helpful suggestions.

Thanks especially to my granddaughter, Summer Andrecht, who designed, typeset, and otherwise made this book suitable for publication.

And finally, special thanks to my publisher/daughter, Polly Meyers, who flattered, cajoled, and pushed me to allow her to reprint this book.

Contents

Illustrations

This

steaming cup
of fragrant brew
holds a message
just for you.

Tea Cup Tales

"There he is!" I told my friend, Maggie, as I studied her teacup in my hands. "Your knight in shining armor! He'll be coming into your life soon. Perhaps in two weeks. But, what's this? He's riding on a chicken?"

Would you like to astound your friends and put a little psychic excitement into your own life? Most of us have some intuitive ability, and tea leaf reading is an easy way to develop it.

There is something fun and magical about reading tea leaves, and it's relaxing to share a cup of tea with friends. We all enjoy interesting stories about ourselves.

Tea also makes us feel good. Studies of tea drinking people indicate that tea enhances the immune system and may even help prevent cancer. Recent research in Japan and the United States shows that tea significantly inhibits the development of many kinds of cancer in mice. Who can say whether it's something in the tea, or the ambiance created by putting on the kettle that creates beneficial health effects? I wonder if mice enjoy their tea parties as much as people do.

My husband, James, and I took a trip to Great Britain this summer. James ended up in a hospital in Wales. It was no fun to have him ill, but the hospital stay was one of our most memorable experiences. Several times a day the tea trolley came around with tea for patients and visitors alike. It certainly did improve the hospital routine.

Americans are discovering what the British have known for a long time, which is the pleasure of tea time. Tea rooms are springing up all over this country and are becoming more popular all the time.

It's enjoyable, but expensive, to visit one of the little tea rooms. Think how much more fun it would be to have tea time in your own home. To add to the enjoyment, you can learn to read the leaves. It's not difficult.

As a child, were you able to spot pictures hidden in the clouds? If so, you have a special talent for *tasseography* — the reading of cups. Tea leaf reading is the easiest and friendliest of the divining arts, but practiced by few. All you need is a vivid imagination and a pot of tea.

Setting the Stage

Making a pot of tea isn't difficult, and with a little time and effort you can make your tea leaf session into a memorable and charming event. If you do a good job reading the leaves, people will remember the event with pleasure, even if they don't quite remember everything you said.

This enchanting experience is fun. So, enjoy it! Set your table with your best tablecloth and a vase of flowers, lovingly arranged. Put out some cookies. Offer lemon, milk, and sugar to accent your flavorful tea. Put on the kettle and invite a friend over. Doesn't that sound delightful?

Actually, I rarely serve tea that way. Most of the time, people drop in unexpectedly and I put on the kettle. If I have cookies, I offer them. Sometimes I have flowers, but seldom a tablecloth. It's still fun.

If you entertain at someone else's party, dress the part. Your clothes can be mood-setting. If you're a woman, wear a long slinky dress with gaudy earrings or gypsy baubles – whatever looks interesting and mysterious.

A man could look dramatic in black slacks and a turtleneck with a gold chain and medallion. Dress to set yourself apart from the rest of the guests. Who would expect a tea leaf reader to look ordinary? Of course, if you do a good job, no one will care what you look like.

The Equipment

The teapot you use to serve the tea is important. If possible, try to find a pot without a strainer in the spout. The purpose of the strainer is to keep the leaves in the pot. You want the leaves to come out.

The prettiest pots all seem to have porcelain strainers built into their spouts. I've searched and searched, and the only pot I've found without a strainer looks like a bean pot. You have to decide whether you want a pretty teapot or a practical one. If your favorite teapot has a strainer, use it. You will just have to spoon out some leaves to put in the cup after you pour the tea. It horrifies my husband when I do this. "That's cheating!" he cries. I don't think it's cheating. It's a little awkward, but in the end it doesn't affect the reading.

Teacups are important too. They should taper gracefully to the base. It doesn't matter how beautifully decorated they are on the outside, just be sure they are plain white inside. It's difficult to read a cup when you can't tell whether you're reading leaves or little flowers painted on the inside of the cup.

Now that you have a teapot and teacups, the next step is to choose a tea that has interesting and easy-to-read leaves. If you can find a tea that smells and tastes good, all the better.

Choosing Your Tea

Black teas are usually the easiest to read. My favorite is Chinese Restaurant tea. It has to be the black tea, however. There is a green Chinese Restaurant tea as well. Green tea is often difficult to read. The leaves are so large they fill the cup and don't tell you much.

I also enjoy flavored black teas such as Apricot and Cherry. The pictures they form are clear and recognizable, and the tea is delicious. Some people have never tasted a good cup of tea. All teas do not taste alike. There is an amazing selection to choose from, and tea hunting can be addictive. If you need a harmless addiction, this could be it.

I've often read that tea should be used shortly after you buy it to enjoy the full rich flavor. Many tea experts admonish you to keep your tea in a tea tin or other airtight container and use it within two weeks to enjoy it at its best.

Lately, I've heard that tea that is kept cool and dry can be stored for up to a year without loss of flavor. That's welcome news to me, because I'm one of those harmless addicts. I have more tea in my cupboard than I could use in two years, let alone two weeks.

Shop around for your teas. I've found some unusually interesting teas at a little Vietnamese grocery store. One that struck my fancy is called Bojenmi. It smells of sandalwood and has a unique flavor. Best of all, the leaves make spectacular pictures.

My daughter-in-law, Mary Ellen, says it tastes like mud and she refuses to drink it. Too bad, the label says it's good for you. Bojenmi may be a little difficult for many of you to find, but you might have fun looking.

Reading labels on these foreign tea boxes can be entertaining. The label of Bojenmi says:

> Particularly good for reducing weight. For female, a regular administration is best possible way to keep their youth and health. For elderly, a regular administration can help them reduce their cholesterol level, thus less liable to hardening of the arteries and coronary disorders. Its refreshing property is of benefit to offensive breath and erosion of lips and tongue.

You'll never see a label like that on a box of Lipton's tea! In the Orient, tea was a medicine before it was a social beverage. Evidently, it still is.

If you still hold doubts about the medicinal value of tea, consider the following information that came from a package of Jasmine tea purchased at the same little Vietnamese grocery store:

> Modern scientific analysis attributes to tea the following eight elements essential to human physiology:

Theine stimulates the circulation, raises the spirits, keeps the mind alert, relieves fatigue, and clears the kidneys of residual poisons.

Tannic acid gets rid of fats, helps digestion, strengthens the spleen, increases the appetite, dissolves alcohol, and relieves nicotine poisoning.

Vitamins increase the elasticity of blood vessels, resist germs, and protect bone growth.

Essential oil stimulates blood circulation, promotes metabolism, and improves tissue function.

Manganese and fluoking improve metabolism, aid sexual activity, and protect the mouth.

Chlorophyll cleanses the blood, prevents aging, and helps keep women attractive.

Hydrochloric acid cures the thyroid and promotes metabolism.

Carbohydrates maintain health, enrich nutrition, and promote long life.

Teas with easy-to-read leaves are widely available. Try to find a flavored tea, such as Apricot or Cherry, or a traditional tea such as black Chinese Restaurant tea, English Breakfast, Earl Grey, Orange Ceylon, Darjeeling, or Constant Comment. Most of these are available in grocery stores, but make sure you buy the loose tea and not tea bags. A tea bag broken open is one of the worst choices. The leaves are fine and powdery. The designs are blurry. You can read it, but it isn't easy.

Almost any loose black tea will work. You may find one you like better than any of these. When reading at a psychic fair one year, I used a cinnamon and spice tea I bought in bulk at a health food store. It was fragrant and delicious. You could smell it all over the room. That may have been why there was a longer line at my booth than at any of the others. Many people who sat to have their leaves read asked, "Do I have to drink it all?"

"A sip or two is enough," I assured them. Then they drained their cups!

Brewing the Tea

Proper Tea

To have leaves to read, you first have to make the tea. Fill the teapot with boiling water to preheat it so it will be warm when you pour the hot tea water into it from the tea kettle. Then bring fresh water to a vigorous rolling boil in your tea kettle. Empty the water out of the now preheated teapot. Add leaves to the teapot – one teaspoon for each cup of water and one for the pot. Next, pour the kettle's boiling water over the leaves in the teapot. Cover and let steep for three to seven minutes before pouring the tea.

This recipe makes good tea; it makes good *strong* tea. The tea gets stronger the longer it sits on all those leaves. After drinking a few cups, the inside of your mouth feels like an old dirty wash rag.

I make tea this way if I'm reading for a large group of people. I keep pouring fresh boiling water over the same leaves in the teapot. The tea doesn't have time to get strong since it is constantly being poured, and there are plenty of leaves in the pot to go around.

Leisurely Tea

If I have one or two friends over and we're enjoying a leisurely cup of tea with good conversation, I make tea this way:

Fill a tea kettle about two-thirds full of water. Bring to a rolling boil. Make sure it's really rolling. Quickly, take the kettle off the burner and hold it over the sink. Toss in a heaping teaspoon of leaves. The water will boil up in the tea kettle and the leaves will appear to explode. The tea leaves and water may boil over, that's why you hold the kettle over the sink. The leaves won't "explode," however, unless the water is boiling vigorously. I think the explosion brings out a little more flavor. If you don't have this experience the first time you try, the tea will still taste good.

Cover the tea kettle when the boiling dies down and steep the leaves for three to five minutes. Look in the kettle. If you see many leaves floating around on the top, pour in a quarter cup of cold water. This will help settle the leaves. You may have to swirl the kettle a couple of times to stir up the leaves when you're ready to pour the tea, but that's better than having too many floating leaves gush out.

I love to explode tea leaves. Unfortunately, I can't get herbal teas to explode. I keep trying, but haven't done it yet.

Reading Herb Teas

You read herb teas, also known as *tisanes,* the same way you read other teas. There's no need to give up this enjoyable pastime if you truly don't care for ordinary tea.

Some herbal teas are easier to read than others. If the herb's leaves are very large, crumble them between your fingers before brewing. Opening tea bags doesn't work any better with herbal teas than with black teas.

I made some orange bergamot tea *(M.P. Citrata)* from some of my own plants. I dried them first, of course. The leaves are coarse, so I crumbled them before I made my tea. It was a good tea to read, and tasted good too. It has a citrus-like flavor and fragrance and belongs to the mint family.

Blackberry leaf tea is another good one to read, and it is delicious. You have to crumble the leaves for easiest reading. It is also good iced. Lemon Thyme is another delicious tea, but the leaves are very light and it takes a long time for them to sink to the bottom of the cup. Many of the herb teas are like this. I've read chamomile tea, but I wouldn't recommend it. While it tastes good, those little flowers are a distraction.

To make herbal tea, prepare the tea water the same as you would for a black tea. After adding the tea to the kettle or pot, let it steep for a few minutes. Then, pour in a quarter cup of cold water to settle the leaves. Let it steep for a few more minutes. The longer it steeps the more leaves will settle. If the leaves haven't fallen enough by the end of five to ten minutes, pour the tea into your teacups and skim off the floaters. You may want to simply use a teapot with a built-in strainer to pour the tea, then use a spoon to scoop out some leaves from the bottom of the pot to add to the cups.

You'll have to experiment with your own favorite teas. Find one you like and practice a lot. As soon as you catch yourself reading the cracks in the ceiling, the grain in the wood paneling, and the markings on your cat, you'll know you can read anything.

History

While you (the reader) and your sitter (the person whose cup you will read) are sipping your tea, you might like to share a little history with her about the art of tea leaf reading.

People have been reading meaning into things since time began. They've read the stars, entrails of animals, rocks, sticks, just about anything. It surprised me to learn that the earliest record of tea leaf reading is relatively recent. It began in a drawing room in eighteenth century England.

Anna, the wife of the Seventh Duke of Bedford, originated the custom of afternoon tea. It may have been in her drawing room that the first cup was read.

Tea came to England in the seventeenth century. Introduced by the Dutch traders, tea was so rare and expensive that only the wealthy could afford it . . . and they kept it locked up so their servants wouldn't steal it.

Tea may seem a benign and insignificant beverage to you, but its history is violent. Since tea was an expensive luxury, smuggling, piracy, and politics were all involved in the tea trade. Remember the Boston Tea Party?

Originally, tea came from China, where it was primarily used as medicine before it was drunk for pleasure. Now, tea is grown in many other countries as well, such as Japan, India, Ceylon, Indonesia, and even parts of the former Soviet Union.

Tea still plays an important role in the life and culture of China. I find it hard to believe that having had tea in their possession so much longer than the rest of us, they didn't notice those little pictures in the cups. Sometimes, especially when using Chinese Restaurant tea, the pictures in the cup look as though they could have come right off an oriental scroll painting.

Seeing those pictures in the cup is the easy part. Attaching meaning to the pictures isn't easy. You need to practice with a list of meanings for reference. Find a patient friend who's willing to let you experiment before you go public.

I've included a list of symbols in this book. It's as complete as I could make it. When I was learning, I had at least half a dozen books. If I couldn't find a meaning in one book that seemed to fit, I'd try another book.

You'll notice that some of the symbols have more than one meaning. Sometimes none of the meanings will fit. Often, a meaning will flash into your mind. This is where intuition comes in. The more you practice, the better you'll get at it. Soon you'll be able to dispense with the books. Then you'll have a skill that will make you even more popular than you already are.

I started reading tea leaves one Christmas. Someone in the family got a book on fortune telling. There were several different methods, but we were already tea drinkers so we didn't need any extra equipment.

The whole family got involved. With the book in one hand and teacup in the other, one member of the family would read until his or her imagination was exhausted. Then he or she would pass the cup to the next person. It was interesting to notice how we each interpreted the pictures differently. One daughter read on a physical level and seemed to intuit health problems. One son read on a spiritual level.

As you become more polished and skillful, you will begin to read for your friends. The result? More friends.

Reading the Leaves

The purpose of this book is to teach you a new skill, a skill that will help you develop the imaginative, or right (as opposed to left), side of your brain. When learning any new skill, you need a few rules to help you get started. Once you learn the basics, you're free to violate them in any way that seems appropriate to you.

Reading the Cup

Notice when your sitter has almost finished her tea. Ask her to leave about a teaspoon of liquid in the bottom of the cup. Then ask her to swirl the cup three times. If the sitter is right handed, swirl counterclockwise; a left-handed sitter will swirl clockwise. When she is finished, have the sitter carefully turn the cup upside down onto a saucer. Ask her to place both hands on the bottom of the cup and make a wish.

When the wish is made, the sitter removes her hands from the bottom of the cup. You then pick up the cup, hold it by the handle, and look inside.

The Four Directions

The four directions are based on your holding the cup by the handle in your left hand. If you hold the cup in your right hand, you must adjust the directions accordingly.

The Four Directions: The area by the handle, held in your left hand, represents the sitter and her home. In the example pictured above, the sitter is from California, so the handle represents west. The side of the cup farthest from you is north. The side opposite the handle is east. The area closest to you is south.

For a Texan, the area nearest the handle would represent her home in the south. Opposite the handle would be north, and so on. Make adjustments in direction depending on where your sitter lives.

Any symbol facing the sitter, or moving toward the handle represents a person or an event coming toward the sitter or being friendly to the sitter. Anything facing away from the sitter (and probably facing you, if the sitter is sitting opposite you) represents someone or something leaving, or the sitter going somewhere.

For example, your sitter from California has an airplane near the rim of the northern side of her cup. The airplane appears to be heading toward the handle, which in this case is her home in the west. You tell her, "You will have a visitor soon from the north."

If the airplane is facing east, away from the sitter's home, and is in the middle of the cup, the sitter herself will take a trip in about two weeks. Depending on other pictures in the cup, it could also represent someone close to her leaving. Perhaps you will see a boy and a book next to the plane. You might guess she has a son going away to school.

Time in the Cup

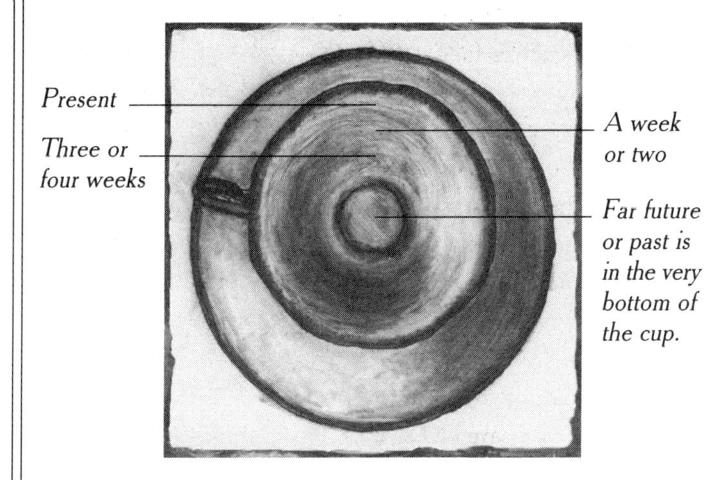

Time in the Cup: The rim always represents the present. The bottom of the cup indicates the future. How far you see into the future depends upon you and your intuition. For example, if you want the future to be four weeks away, then the point halfway down the inside of the cup represents about two weeks into the future. If the future is four months away, then the midpoint of the cup represents half that, or two months.

If you want to read the past, you will call the bottom of the cup the distant past while the rim is still the present. Most people want to hear about the present and the future and not the past. However, one cup I read had crosses and a church in the bottom of the cup. It looked like a graveyard to me. How could I read something helpful in that cup? It looked depressing. Not knowing what to say, I questioned the sitter. She told me her two daughters had gone back to South Carolina to attend their father's funeral. She and their father had been separated for many years. Although the funeral had taken place several months before, all she could talk and think about was the funeral. There was nothing else in the cup. It was as if she was trapped in the past and couldn't break out of it. The leaves showed regret, sorrow, and pain. I tried to relieve her, but she wasn't ready to end her mourning.

Reading the Leaves

Now that you have some background and some guidelines, it's time to read the cup. You usually begin reading at the rim and move around the cup clockwise from level to level until you come to the bottom. Yet rules are made to be broken. If some other method works better for you, do it your way.

Hold the cup in both hands. Study it carefully. Don't be in a hurry to say anything. Assume a dreamy, relaxed attitude. Put your mind in neutral while you turn the cup slowly. I suggest that you turn it first one way, then another. The same leaves looked at from different angles form different pictures. It's perfectly legitimate to interpret all the angles.

At first the leaves look like leaves. You will think, "Now what have I gotten myself into?" Don't panic. The pictures will come. Some will suddenly become clear and you'll wonder how you missed them. Take plenty of time. If there are six people clamoring to have their leaves read, relax, you'll give them the same attention.

Look for one outstanding picture to start your reading with. If certain pictures dominate the cup, you can be sure they dominate the mind of your sitter.

Overall Picture

You can tell a lot about your sitter by the way the leaves are scattered around the cup.

Cup 1: Obsessive

In Cup #1 all the leaves are in one big pile. In this example, your sitter has one big problem. If the leaves are piled in the bottom of the cup, she's concerned about something that will happen in the future, unless she's a person who lives in the past. As I said, the bottom of the cup can represent either the future or the past. You won't usually read the past, since most people want to know what's *going* to happen. They already know what *has* happened. But, you will sometimes get a feeling that the leaves represent the past. If you feel this, say so. That's what intuition is.

Let's assume that the sitter is concerned about an upcoming problem. Study the pile. See if you can see anything there that might indicate a way out of her problem. Suppose you see a shovel on top of the pile. You could say, "It's going to take hard work, but you will be able to dig your way out of this."

It constantly amazes me the way people put their memories, emotions, and states of mind into their cups. I'm convinced that there is a higher power in each of us. We are not consciously aware of this higher part, but it is aware of us. It is constantly struggling to get messages through to us, messages that will help us lead happier and more orderly lives. You've had hunches, haven't you? Those are messages getting through.

One morning, my husband (who is a chronic worrier), woke up more worried than usual. He was going around and around in his head, trapped by one big worry. He handed me his cup.

I had to laugh. There was one big "worry-ball" of tea leaves with a head sticking out of the top and two arms waving frantically. It was so obvious that he laughed too. I didn't have to interpret the leaves for him. If he'd drunk another cup of tea and I'd read his tea leaves again, I would have found a similar picture. I know from experience that that would happen until he changed his frame of mind.

Cup 2: Scattered

The entire inside of Cup #2 is spattered with leaves. The sitter is as scattered and busy as the cup looks. This person has too many projects. She is also an energetic, stimulating person who is perhaps a little exhausting. You might warn her to slow down. While your sitter might not listen, later she will probably tell you that she wished she had.

Cup 3: Balanced

Cup #3 has clear pictures that are evenly balanced throughout the cup. This may indicate that the sitter is a well-balanced person. As you read for family and friends whose personalities are familiar to you, you will begin to recognize personality patterns in cups. These patterns will also hold true for people whom you don't know.

Reading Symbols in the Leaves

Tea leaf patterns are like dreams. They belong to the person who forms them. So keep checking with your sitter. Some symbols are personal to her.

Ordinarily, if I see a dog in a cup, I think *faithful friend.* What I might not know is that the sitter has had a bad experience with a dog and may be deathly afraid of them. So, proceed cautiously. There might be other symbols in the cup that would tip you off to this, but, as a beginner, you might not recognize them. So, again, check with the sitter. Get the sitter involved in her reading. "What does a dog mean to you?" you might ask.

Symbols occur on three levels. The first is the personal level. These symbols result from personal experiences and are not applicable to most other people. Next is the general level. Symbols at this level represent the ideas or situations most people think of when they see a symbol or hear a word. Last is the mythic or fairy tale level, what psychoanalyst Carl Jung calls the *collective unconscious.*

Call the symbols as you recognize them. Suppose you see what looks like a little girl in a sunbonnet in a young man's cup. You know he's too young to have his own little girl. Or is he? Check. "I see a little girl in a sunbonnet. Does that have special meaning for you?" you would ask.

He may say, "Oh, that's my grandmother. I have a picture

of her as a little girl. She's wearing a sunbonnet."

You then find out he's expecting a visit from her. Perhaps there is an airplane, halfway down the cup, coming from the south and heading toward the handle. His grandmother lives in the south. She plans to visit in two weeks.

Sometimes, the person you are reading for is as puzzled as you by the symbols. Then, using your imagination and the list of symbols in this book, start asking questions.

The leaves speak the truth. If you can't always read them, don't give up. It takes time and practice. Remember, you don't have to read every leaf. Just pick out the ones that seem to make a picture.

As you do this and become more comfortable with it, you will find yourself talking. The words will spill out and you won't know for sure where they are coming from. You've reached the intuitive level of your brain. What you say from this level will usually be most meaningful to your sitter. It may not seem so at the time you say it, but will later.

Because the leaves speak the truth, people are open to you when they allow you to read their leaves. They are vulnerable and sensitive. This puts great responsibility on you to do them no harm. You will find that you are open to your sitter as well. The two of you become almost one. Tuning in this way generates a warm and affectionate tie between you, at least for the duration of the reading.

This happens whether you want it to or not. I was trapped once into reading for someone whom I didn't like. Before the reading was over, however, I found that my feelings had changed. I generated so much insight into the woman's problems that I only felt love for her by the end.

Tea leaf reading is more than fun and games. It's a way to develop compassion and understanding for other people. If you don't find this true for yourself, you should probably find another hobby.

Feeling as I do about the person whose cup I hold, I choose my words carefully. My desire is to help the person I'm reading for see her problems in as clear a light as possible so she can find her own way out of them. I want to give my friend hope, to promise excitement and pleasant surprises, and generally lift her spirits. I want my friend to discover unsuspected talents and beguiling aspects of her personality.

You may think that's a big goal. How can anyone do that? I can't explain exactly how, but the words come tumbling out and *they* do it.

I constantly surprise myself with the number of "hits" I make. I once saw a confederate hat in a man's cup. It didn't seem to be related to anything else. I was puzzled and said, "I see a confederate hat in your cup."

"Of course," he said, "I collect them. I'm going to pick up a new one this afternoon." He was not as surprised as I was.

A word of caution! You may not need it, but I'll give it anyway. Never predict death or any unavoidable disaster. You might be wrong. You may be right, but is that a good reason to cause premature sorrow? You could be wrong, too.

You *can* warn of impending danger. You can suggest to your sitter that she be especially cautious during a specified time. A little hint of danger can add some spice to a reading, as long as the sitter feels that she has some control over it.

There will be times when something in the cup looks ominous to you. "Should I or shouldn't I say something?" you wonder. Handle it carefully.

An example: I see an uprooted oak tree. An oak tree represents stability and strength. I begin by asking the obvious: "Are you planning to remove a tree from your yard?"

If we can't find any simple explanation for the uprooted oak, I say, "There is something in your life, or coming into it, which will tax your strength. It will take a lot out of you if you let it. Try to get some extra rest and take especially good care of yourself so you'll have all the energy you need to carry it off splendidly."

Just about everyone has something taxing in their lives. And most of us need to be encouraged to take better care of ourselves. Coming from the objective teacup, your sitter might pay attention.

Making Predictions

Be aware that some people listening to your predictions will attempt to make them come true. Be careful with any one who is suggestible.

My youngest son, Arthur, and his wife, Mary Ellen, have

three cats because of what I saw in their cups. I saw kittens in both their cups one night. That was all the encouragement they needed to go out and find a kitten. The next time I read their cups, I still saw kittens. Sure enough, they got another cat.

When I saw a third cat in my son's cup, I said, "Don't go looking for another cat! This one is looking for you."

I was talking to Arthur not long after in front of his brother Jim's house. To my utter amazement, a little silver-striped kitten streaked down the street and leaped into Arthur's arms.

He didn't want to give up the kitten that had chosen him. But he didn't want to take someone else's cat. Arthur knocked on doors all up and down the street. No one claimed the kitten. My son had his third cat.

In spite of the cups, Mary Ellen was a little perturbed. Two cats were enough! She finally decided it was fate and has accepted the kitten.

I love it when my predictions come true, but I don't let it go to my head. As you can see by the story of the cats, some people will go to great lengths to make a prediction come true. Other people have a tendency to fill in the details. A sitter might give you credit for things you know you didn't say.

I may say, "I see a capital A. It's someone with quite a bit of money because the letter is surrounded by small dots."

"Oh, that's Uncle Andrew. He's my rich uncle." The sitter has supplied his name, but later she will be sure you did.

Recently, I ran into a friend whose leaves I had read several months before. She asked, "Remember what you told me about the butterflies?"

I didn't. At the risk of spoiling my image, I asked, "What did I tell you about the butterflies?"

"You told me to expect some butterflies in my life," she said. Butterflies mean harmless, frivolous pleasures. My friend is a serious businesswoman not given to frivolous pleasures. When I had told her I saw her going dancing and having a marvelous time, she had said, "Nonsense! I haven't gone dancing in years." But she did. She went dancing with an old friend she hadn't seen in years and had a marvelous, lighthearted time.

Another woman reminded me that I had seen a maple leaf in her cup. I had told her, "Something or someone important is coming to you from Canada." Shortly afterwards, she met a woman from Canada who soon became her best friend.

Sometimes, a sitter will leave too much liquid in the cup and when she turns it over all the leaves will spill into the saucer. When this happens, I expect she's daring me to find her out.

One lady did just this. I looked into her cup and there was not a leaf in sight. "Well," I said, "you are washing the past right out of your life."

"You're exactly right," she said.

So I read her saucer. I saw her taking a trip south – perhaps planning to move to the south. I saw hats and boots and bridges. All indications of change. She assured me that that was her intention.

There is another thing I should tell you. What you read in the cup is often a reflection of what is going on in the person's mind and life at the time. This means that your predictions are based on the idea that events will continue to go as expected. But, things *don't* always go as expected, so occasionally your predictions may not come true. Fortunately, most people forget predictions that don't come true and only remember the dramatic ones that *do* come to pass.

I find that reading tea leaves is a remarkably effective way to keep in touch with my friends and family. Remember my friend Maggie whose cup revealed a knight in shining armor riding on a chicken? We puzzled over that picture, alternately amused and confused.

A chicken, to most of us, means cowardice. Yet, we can't overlook the obvious. Her knight in shining armor might be a chicken rancher. Then Maggie mentioned a brothel in Nevada referred to as *The Chicken Ranch. That* gave me a start. But the Nevada Chicken Ranch had no part in my reading. I'd read for Maggie many times before, and we both knew I'd made more hits than misses. Still, we couldn't figure out what a knight riding a chicken might mean, and it was months before we unraveled the mystery.

Shortly after the reading, Maggie met a very attractive gentleman. He helped her get a job she wanted and needed. He took her under his *wing* and seemed to answer her every prayer. It wasn't until she was deeply involved with him that his weaknesses came out. She found him failing her in one situation after another. He was afraid to defend her when she was fired from the very job he helped her get. He was *chicken.* She finally realized that she was in a dead-end situation and got herself, painfully, out of it. All this was shown symbolically in her teacup, but the symbols' meanings weren't clear until afterward.

What value was the reading? Perhaps it helped her recognize the situation sooner than she would have otherwise. At the time, she had needed the job, and perhaps she had also needed the experience.

Tea leaf patterns are like dreams. They belong to the sitter who creates them. The famous dream analyst Carl Jung taught that we are all connected in some way with a great pool of infinite knowledge – the collective unconscious. When the barriers of the mind are down, as in dreams or any relaxed state such as you will lapse into when you read the leaves, you tap into this great source of knowledge. At this level you know all there is to know. The only problem is that this knowledge comes to you in symbols. If you can just learn to interpret symbols correctly, you'll know everything.

Fortunately, no one knows everything. But we all know a little bit and can learn more. The more I practice reading the leaves, the more often I amaze myself and entertain my friends with exciting predictions for their future.

Before you end your tea leaf session, be sure to look for good luck signs so that you can tell your sitter that her wish will come true. You usually will be able to do that, and it is a pleasant way to end the reading.

In the pages that follow, I have included some sample cups for you to practice with and an exhaustive list of symbols.

As you read more and more teacups, you will come up with meanings of your own and depend less and less on my list. Jung said this about dreams, "Learn as much as you can about interpreting the symbols. Then forget the symbols and read the dreams."

So I say to you: Learn as much as you can about interpreting the symbols, then forget the symbols and read the leaves.

Examples

Sample Cups

The following pages show some sample cups that I have read. Try to interpret them yourself for practice. Remember to look at the cups from different angles. Then look at my interpretations. You won't necessarily see the same things I do. Very likely you won't.

In one of the cups I saw a vintage airplane. My daughter-in-law, Mary Ellen, looked at it and said, "That looks like a witch to me."

I said, "Great!" The idea is to see *something.* Then interpret what you see. Your reading has to come from within you. Now is the time to see how good your imagination is. Have fun!

Cup A: Domestic Problems

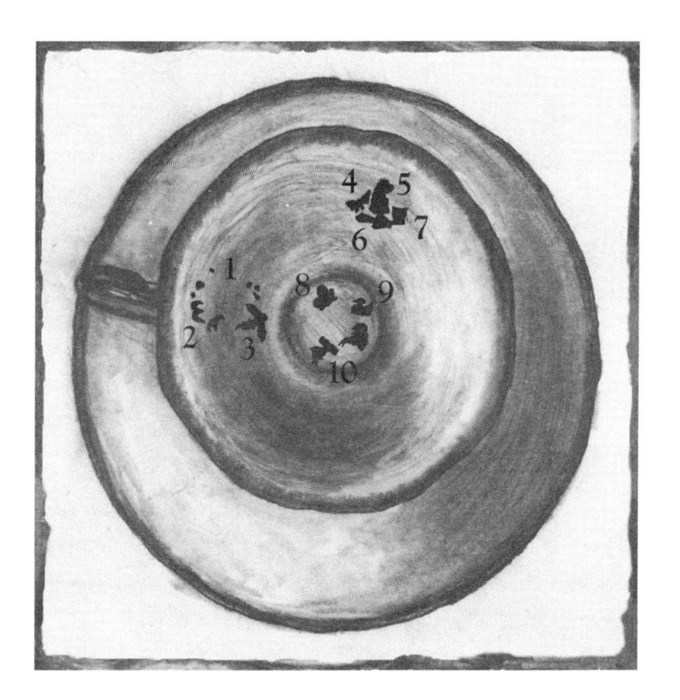

Start your reading at the handle. The handle represents the sitter and her home. Read clockwise around the cup.

1. **Incomplete circle.**
2. **Two hawks.** Hawks represent jealousy.
3. **Person in a boat.** Boat represents travel; water represents the emotions.

Interpretation: You're involved in a circle of jealousy. I see you breaking the emotional spell, rowing away from it.

4. **Butterfly.** Harmless fun.
5. **Bear**. A journey.
6. **Spade**. Hard work.
7. **Pail.** Hard work in marriage, but much love.

   Interpretation: You'll be taking a trip north, within two or three weeks. It will be a business trip, work, but you'll be taking your spouse. It will give you a chance to be together and enjoy some harmless fun. In addition, it will give you the opportunity to do some hard work on your marriage – work that is worth the effort because there is much love there. The outcome should be very good.

On the bottom of the cup, a little look into the future:

8. **Frog.** Beware of self-importance.
9. **Duck.** Persistent effort.
10. **Someone lecturing to another person who is being hit on the head.**

    Interpretation: Your persistent efforts will bring you success that could go to your head. However, you have a good friend who will make sure this doesn't happen.

Cup B: Business Cup

1. **Vintage airplane.** A plane, heading toward the handle, means a visitor.
   Interpretation: A visitor from the north. Because the plane is old, it represents something from the past. Your visitor will be an old friend.
2. **Shovel.** Hard work, digging in.

Interpretation: The old friend will revive memories that will cause you to do some digging into the past. Your research will carry you in a northeasterly direction.

3. **Duck.** Persistent efforts needed, involving money.
   Interpretation: The result of digging into the past will involve you in a money-making venture. That duck has an exceptionally long neck. You are apt to have your neck stuck far out on this deal. Success will require persistence on your part.
4. **Jet airplane.** A trip.
   Interpretation: This is definitely a modern plane. You will be taking a trip south soon. This trip will probably be to wind up some details of your money-making venture.
5. **Mushroom.** Growth and expansion. An obstacle.
   Interpretation: All you efforts will result in growth for you. You have an obstacle to overcome and the effort to do so will bring an increase in your personal growth, the growth of your business, or both.
6. **Boot.** New direction, new effort.
7. **Three dots.** Money.
   Interpretation: Your persistent efforts will result in a totally different outcome than you expect, but will bring you money.

Cup C: Get Life in Order

1. **Person with heavy burden.**
2. **Restraining hand.**

   Interpretation: You have so much work to do and so many things to straighten out. You'd like to throw over the whole thing and go far away. (Notice how close you, the figure with the heavy burden, are to the rim of the cup?) You're close to the limit of what you can take. However, the restraining hand of your conscience is holding you to the task at hand.

3. **Sailor.** Dreams of distant places.
4. **Boat.** Travel or refuge in times of trouble.

   Interpretation: Daydreaming about trips to faraway romantic places is your refuge. This is how you mentally escape, even though you physically stay where you are.
5. **Hen.** Domestic tranquillity.
6. **Person sorting through piles of things.**
7. **Person packing a suitcase.**

   Interpretation: Your happiness at home makes your overwhelming burdens at least bearable. You realize that you can't go on like this much longer, so you settle down to the business of sorting through your obligations. You put them in order of priority, throw out whatever you can, and get out from under these responsibilities. You realize that you got yourself into this mess and no one else will get you out. Then you become free to pack your suitcase for that romantic trip.

Cup D: Restrictions

1. **Puritan.** Strict religious outlook.
2. **Small girl.** Childhood (for female sitter).

   Interpretation: You had a strict religious upbringing. It was so strict that it keeps you from enjoying even simple pleasures. You feel guilty.
3. **Bull's head.** A stubborn, strong-willed person. Perhaps a Taurus.

4. **Dancer.** Exuberance.

   Interpretation: The dancer is someone who really cares about you and wants you to release these old inhibitions and enjoy life more fully. He or she won't take *no* for an answer.
5. **Children fighting.**

   Interpretation: Two children in your head are causing you turmoil. The child that wants to enjoy innocent pleasures and the child who was brought up so strictly are forcing you to some decision.
6. **Rooster.** Something to crow about.
7. **Rabbit.** Timidity.
8. **Chick hatching.** New life.

   Interpretation: You'll have something to crow about because you decide to let go of old, outworn beliefs. You're a little bit hesitant at first, but once you make up your mind, a whole new world opens to you.

Cup E: Workaholic

1. **Butterfly.** Innocent pleasures.
2. **Swan.** A contented life.
3. **Flying fish.** A fish with wings means swift rewards.
4. **Pitcher.** Success through hard work.

Interpretation: You aren't happy unless you're in the thick of accomplishing things. You thrive on hard work and are content with your life because you also find time for innocent pleasures. Rewards come quickly as a result of your hard work. You're successful and lucky.

5. **Two hats.** New possibilities and probable success.
6. **Big tangle with a person rising up out of it.**
7. **Another tangle, this one with an airplane caught in it.**

Interpretation: Wearing two hats, you will find yourself involved in two new projects. Both will bring success. Even though you get deeply involved in projects, you are able to lift yourself above the hassle for spiritual refreshment. You would like to take a trip east, but your work is holding you back. With your ability and good luck, you will find a way to make the trip.

Cup F: Self-Doubt

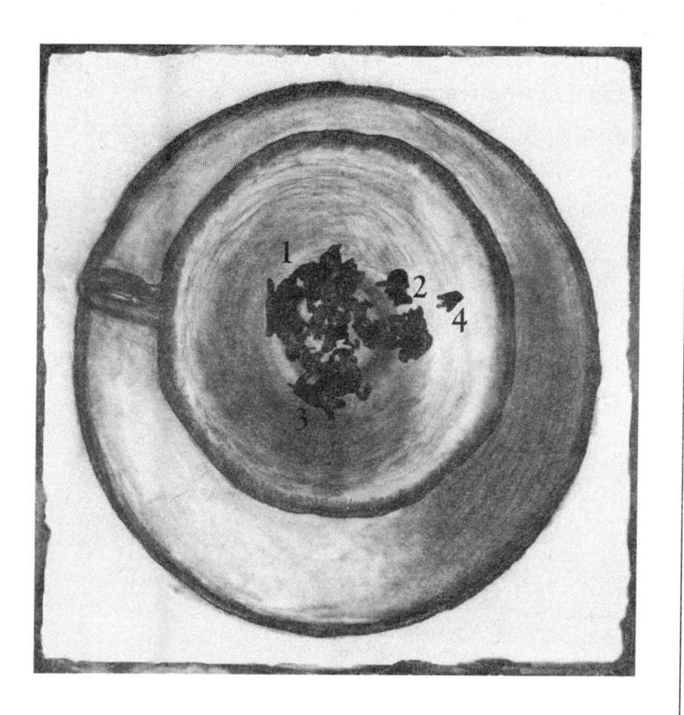

1. **Tangle.** A big ball of worry.
2. **Person in a baseball cap.**

   Interpretation: These tea leaves show your present state of mind, with a hint at the future. You are the figure in the baseball cap, which makes sense because you have just started a baseball-related business and are now wondering if that was a wise thing to do. [The sitter told me of his new business prior to my reading his tea leaves.] The mess means you are worrying about the future. You couldn't have made it much plainer! You're looking down and can't see anything but the mess you think you're in.

3. **Jackass.** A foolish person or situation.
4. **Crown.** Honor and respect. Great abundance. Great success. Your wish will come true.

   Interpretation: Near your head is a crown. If you'd just look up and put things in perspective, you'd realize that you have the potential for great success.

Cup G: A Balanced Life

1. **Vase/Grecian urn.** Architecture. Classics. Peace of mind.
2. **Crown of laurel leaves.** Valor. Victory. Control of a situation.

   Interpretation: The symbol of the Grecian urn indicates an interest in architecture. Around your head a wreath of laurel leaves tells me you're in control. You tell people what to do and they do it.

3. **Boomerang.** Returned obligations. Something returning to you, either for good or ill.
   Interpretation: The boomerang means that everything good you do comes back at you.
4. **Two birds on a branch.** Flight. A trip. Good news.
   Interpretation: Two birds on a branch tell me that you're planning a trip. One of the birds is eager to leave the nest. The other one is holding back. Is there some reason you are reluctant to leave? Determination will drive you to go anyway. It's a test of character for you. You will pass the test.
5. **Seesaw.** Balance and perspective.
   Interpretation: I see a seesaw, which means that you're succeeding in balancing your many accomplishments and interests.
6. **Fish.** A wish that comes true.
   Interpretation: You have a fish in your cup, one of the best possible signs. You will get your wish, whatever it is, and all will go well with you.

Cup H: A Mother's Cup

1. **Bird.** Good luck. Guidance.
2. **Fork.** A decision. Two ways to go.
3. **Squirrel wearing a hat.** Business. Pragmatism.

   Interpretation: The big bird indicates that you possess good luck, guidance, and leadership qualities. The fork in the bird's beak indicates that you have to make an important decision. Below the bird is a squirrel wearing a hat. The decision is about business.

4. **Wagon.** A slow journey. A heavy load.
   Interpretation: The wagon below the squirrel seems to be spreading its back wheels. You wonder if your business will take you into other countries, or if you will accidently take on too heavy a load.
5. **Skier and mountain.** Hard work. An upward climb.
6. **Flag.** Success or failure. A journey to the top.
   Interpretation: There is a skier climbing up a mountain. He carries a flag, which can mean disaster or triumph. Climbing the mountain is hard work, it also means that you are gambling that you will make it to the top.
7. **Flower.** You will get your wish.

Cup I: A Grandmother's Cup

1. **Boy on skates.**
2. **Flashlight.** Vision. Insight.
3. **Mushroom.** An obstacle to growth.

Interpretation: A boy on skates has turned one foot out from under him: One of your children or grandchildren concerns you deeply. You see him flying out into space with no goal and no plan. The flashlight shows that you want to help light his path so he can see what he is doing, yet the mushroom indicates that he alone can bring about this growth.

4. **Finger pointing.** You have been singled out.
5. **Oriental figure.** The Far East. Asian culture.
6. **A package.** A gift.

   Interpretation: A finger pointing is a sign that you have been singled out for something special. Below the finger is an oriental figure, and behind him is a package, which indicates that he has a gift for you, a gift of knowledge coming from the Orient.

7. **Bowl.** A surprise.
8. **Sombrero.** Mexico.

   Interpretation: A bowl means you will receive a surprise. A sombrero may indicate a trip to Mexico or that something of Mexico is in your future.

9. **Dots.** Money. Coins.

   Interpretation: Little dots are money, which you will receive from several sources.

10. **Arrow.** Many interests. A single direction or goal.
11. **Tricorn.** Three sided symbol.

    Interpretation: A tricorn indicates that you wear three hats, meaning you have three compelling interests which are divided equally. The arrow means that your interests should be brought together to make sure you will hit your mark.

12. **Heart.** Love.

    Interpretation: The heart indicates great love in your life.

Cup J: Scattered Interests

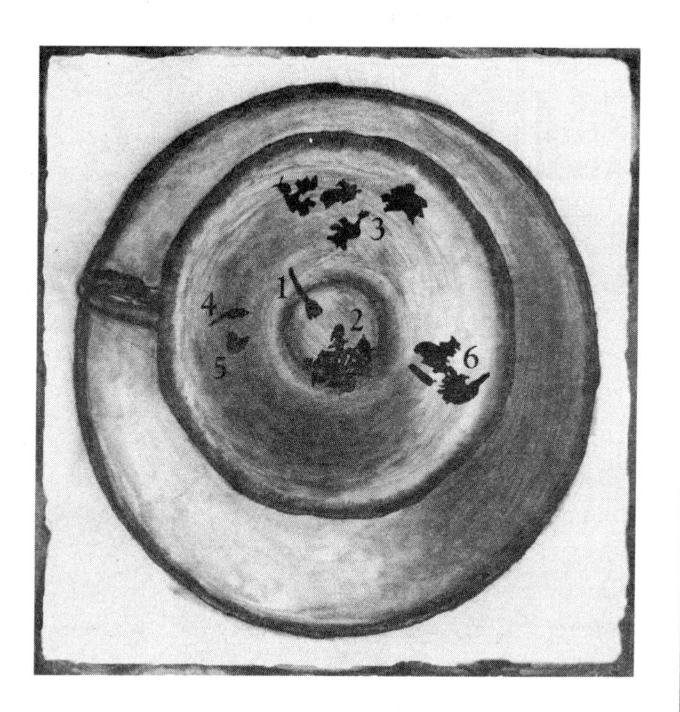

1. **Broom.** Sweeping out the old.
2. **A person emerging from a pile of leaves.** Clutter. An outworn situation. Rebirth.

   Interpretation: You have many interests and talents – so many, in fact, that if you will notice the broom in the bottom of the cup and the head and shoulders coming out of a big pile of leaves, you will realize that you are going to have to clear out a few from your life. You will have to sweep out the clutter and make some choices.

3. **People bearing gifts.** Gifts, repayments, good fortune.
4. **Pen.** Writing. News.
5. **Book.** Reading and /or writing. New information coming your way. Education.
   Interpretation: A pen and a book indicate that you may begin a new writing project or take educational classes. Perhaps you read a lot.
6. **Person at a stove.** Cooking up plots. New projects. Home life.
   Interpretation: You're always cooking up something, and are often too busy to take stock of what is going on around you. Slow down and concentrate on one thing at a time. If not, you will have to crash and learn your lessons the hard way.

This reading was of my own teacup, and I didn't even listen to myself! Shortly after the reading, I came down with shingles and had to stay home and slow down. The moral is: When you read your own cup, pay attention.

Cup K: Talent and Charisma

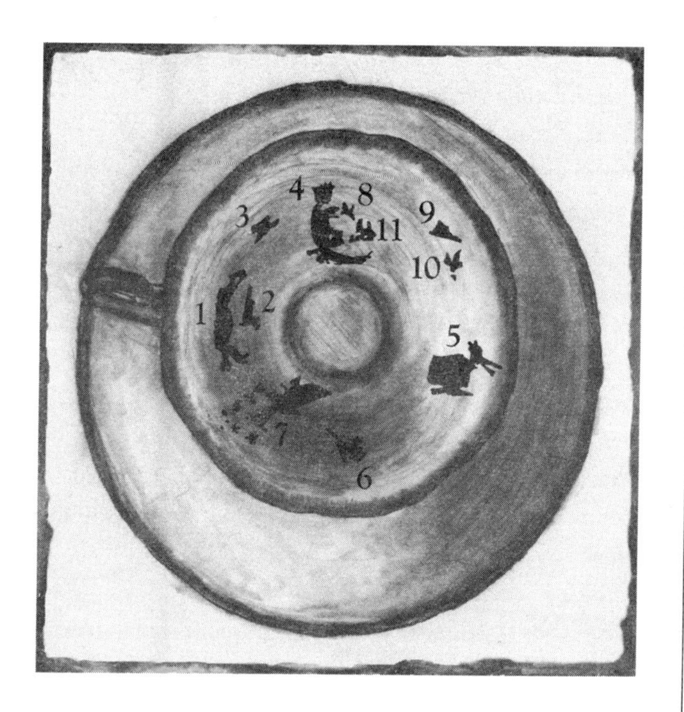

1. **Person leaping over gun.**
2. **Gun.** An argument.
3. **Hat.** New possibilities and probable success.

Interpretation: Person leaping over gun. You'll bend over backward to avoid an argument, but this is one you'll have to meet head on. Once you do, it will all work out for the best and open up new possibilities pointing toward success.

4. **Person wearing a crown.** Honor, respect, wishes will come true.
   Interpretation: The seated figure with the crown is you. Others sit at your feet and pay homage.
5. **Rabbit bearing a gift.** Rabbits signify timidity.
   Interpretation: Although you have a tremendous amount of talent, ability, and intelligence, the rabbit denotes that inside you are really shy. You have to make a great effort to overcome this shyness. The rabbit carrying a gift means that the shyness is a gift. Because of it you can relate to other people's problems with compassion and understanding.
6. **Bouquet.** Love and happiness.
7. **Stars around an angel holding a bouquet of flowers.** Good luck and spiritual consolation.
   Interpretation: A bouquet of flowers portends love and happiness. You are divinely protected and will have sparkling good luck. You have spiritual depth and understanding.
8. **Airplane.** A trip, visitor, or promotion.
9. **Shoe.** A change, probably of work.
10. **Fleur-de-lis.** Something French.
11. **Seated figure reading.**
    Interpretation: I assume that you are the seated figure and the fleur-de-lis and the plane mean that because of your work, you will be lecturing in France before the year is out.

Cup L: A Teenager's Cup

1. **Small dots.** A small amount of money.
2. **Man in hat.**

   Interpretation: The small dots indicate money. Some is given to you, some you will earn. The money you will earn is near the man in the hat. Hats mean new possibilities and potential honors.

3. **Two people in an argument or debate.**
   Interpretation: Below the man in the hat are two people discussing or debating. The man in the hat is watching the debate with great interest. It's a fairly even match, but you are coming out ahead (you are the figure nearest the handle) since the image of you is more defined.
4. **Queen on a throne.**
5. **Airplane.** Someone coming to visit.
   Interpretation: A Queen sits on a throne in the south side of the cup. Below her and supporting her is an airplane coming towards you. Someone with power and authority is coming to you from the south for advice or for something only you can give.
6. **Frying pan.** Something's cooking.
   Interpretation: A frying pan means something very interesting is developing that involves you.
7. **Airplane.** A journey.
8. **Rose.** Artistic success. Friendship.
   Interpretation: Your journey may involve your art, creativity, or a friend.

Cup M: A Twelve Year Old's Cup

1. **Cap.** A need for caution.
2. **Gloves.** Justice will be done.
3. **Dots.** Money.
4. **Candle.** A revelation.

Interpretation: This cup is full of good signs and a few warnings. The cap is a warning to be careful; the glove assures you that justice will be done. The situation concerns money that you may lose. If so, it will be found again. Have patience. The candle means a sudden revelation. It seems to go with the cap, gloves, and dots. Probably you will suddenly remember what happened to the money. It isn't lost at all.

5. **Person riding a bull.** Bull is stubbornness, possibly a Taurus.
6. **Hand-in-victory sign.**
7. **Acorn.** Success.

   Interpretation: You are riding the bull and goading him with a stick. Your stubbornness in pursuing your goals is tremendous, and noting the string of dots following this figure, your persistence will result in money. The victory sign indicates that you are exuberant over your winning against great odds. The acorn is another indication of your success. It also shows that you have a strong character and many abilities that will unfold as you grow older.
8. **Cat.** False friends or a need for independence.
9. **Bird.** Good news.
10. **Mailbox.** A message.

    Interpretation: The cat could mean false friends, but in this instance, it is next to a bird, so it could mean good news. The message will offer an opportunity to become a little more independent and will arrive in the mail.
11. **Boomerang.** Something coming back to you.

    Interpretation: The boomerang means you must be careful

of what you say about your friends. No matter what they say about you, or what you may hear they say about you, don't say anything mean about them. Your words will come back and hit you.

12. **Log.** Ambitions cut off.
    Interpretation: The log indicates that when things are going your way a little disappointment may hit you harder than it should. Be philosophical. You can't win them all. Just be aware that disappointments are part of life.
13. **Rising leaf.** A tea leaf that appears to stand on its end or protrude up out of the cup is a warning to pay attention to what is important to you.
14. **Person.** Probably yourself.
    Interpretation: A rising leaf is a rare symbol in a cup. I see this as a strong warning not to let ambition come before the people and things that are really important to you.
15. **Hare.** Quick decision and action required.
16. **Purse.** Money.
    Interpretation: Are you worried about losing something precious? The hare behind you is a warning that only a quick decision and a change of plans will save you. The purse represents money. My interpretation is that you've let money become too important to you. It's time to put money in its proper place.

Signs and Symbols

In this section, I have given you some general signs and symbols, followed by an alphabetized, comprehensive list of symbols for those of you who want to get a little more out of your tea leaf reading. They will allow for more subtle and precise interpretations, as well as more stimulation for your own imagination.

You will find some of the symbols contradictory. Look to the overall feeling of the cup and especially to the surrounding symbols before choosing your meaning. Better yet, turn your imagination loose and say whatever pops into your head. Have fun!

General Signs

Changes. Archway, bridge, car, hat.
Danger. Flag, hawk, scythe, snake, vulture.
Gift. Basket, jewelry.
Good luck. Angel, circle, clover, egg, fairy, feather, fish, flower, horseshoe, river, spoon.
Good news. Bird, wings.
Love. Heart.
Marriage. Bell, chain, heart, pail, ring.
Misfortune. Bat, cloud, cross, rat, weapon.
Money. Dots, leaves, purse.
Success. Acorn, apple, beehive, boat, coin, crown, fruit, necklace, whale.

Comprehensive List

A

Abbey. Unnecessary worry.
Ace.
Clubs. A letter.
Diamonds. A gift.
Hearts. Love.
Spades. A large building.
Acorn. Success in all endeavors. The promise of great things to come.

Airplane. A trip. A promotion. A rise to new heights. Perhaps risk is involved. Success follows discouragement.

Alligator. Treachery.

Anchor. Stability after turmoil. Travel. Love and constancy.

Angel. Good news. Protection. Spiritual consolation.

Ankle. Ambitious but unstable.

Ants. Perseverance. Thrift. Industry.

Anvil. Continuing effort needed for success.

Apple. Success in business. Desire for a better position in life. Possibility of marital discord. A time to be especially gracious to spouse. *See* ***Fruit.***

Apron. New friends.

Archway. New opportunities. A journey to foreign parts.

Arrow. Many interests. You should choose a definite direction to succeed in your goal.

Attire. Your life will change for the better.

Axe. Mastery of a problem. Trouble surmounted.

B

Baby. New interest. An addition to the family. Small worries. Innocence. Be guided by one young and innocent.

Bag. Holds a surprise. Could be a trap, look to surrounding symbols. *See* ***Bowl.***

Bagpipes. Disappointments. Trouble in home and business. Could represent a friend or relative of Scottish descent.

Ball. Restlessness. Fun and recreation concerns someone involved in sport. Variable fortunes await you.

Barrel. A party. Fun.

Basin. Trouble at home.

Basket. A good sign. A gift. You have the faculty of making the most of what you have.

Surrounded by small dots. Money will come.

With flowers. If flowers are in the basket, happiness is in store.

Bat. A warning. A disappointment. Plots and false friends. Fear of authority. Disappointing journey.

Bath. Disappointment.

Bayonet. Illness or accident. Someone will make a sharp remark about you.

Beans. Money troubles.

Bear. A journey. Delays will cause you trouble.

Bed. Need for a rest. Laziness. A messy or disorganized mind. Look to surrounding symbols.

Bee. A busy time coming. Business success.

In a swarm. Success with a group of people.

Beehive. Business success.

Surrounded by swarming bees. Considerable success.

Beetle. Involvement in some difficult undertaking, but luck is with you.

Bell. A summons, you will be needed. Unexpected news. A wedding. A promotion. Joy.

Bellow. Your interests blow hot and cold. Your plans may meet with reverses.

Bird. Good news. Good luck. Uplifting ideas. Guidance.

Leadership. Insight. *See* ***Dove, Hawk, Raven, Swallow, Swan, Vulture.***

Flying. News will come quickly by letter or phone. A lucky journey.

Bird cage.

Closed door. Restrictions, limitations, and frustration.

Open door. Expect happiness in love, obstacles passing.

Bird nest. Happiness in love and home.

Bishop. Good fortune on its way.

Boat. Travel or a visit from friends. A refuge in time of trouble, probably emotional trouble.

Book. A quest for knowledge. Education. Reading and/or writing.

Closed. A delay. It could represent a student. Litigation.

Open. Success in a new venture.

Boomerang. Beware that what you put out will come back to you.

Boot. Success. Steps in a new direction. It might represent Italy. *See* ***Shoes.***

Bottle. Good luck and prosperity.

One. Indicates pleasure.

Several. Could be illness.

Bouquet. Love and happiness. *See* ***Flower.***

Bow. Good luck. Flirtation. Scandal.

Bowl. A surprise. *See* ***Bag.***

Boy. A child. Innocence. Childhood.

Bracelet. A gathering of friends. Perhaps a marriage. *See* ***Jewelry.***

Branch.

With leaves. A birth.

Bare. A disappointment.

Bread. Do not squander your money or you will be in trouble.

Bridge. An opportunity leads to success.

Broom. A clean sweep. New beginnings. Small worries disappear.

Buckle. To succeed, you must work hard.

Bugle. Blow your own horn, no one will do it for you.

Building. New home or job.

Bull. Stubbornness. Hot air. Someone whose astrological sun sign is Taurus.

Buoy. Do not give up hope, all will turn out well.

Butterfly. Frivolous, but innocent, pleasure.

Surrounded by small dots. Frittering away money.

C

Cabbage. Jealousy.

Cage. Marriage. A proposal. Beware a loveless marriage.

Cake. A party or celebration. A delightful and unexpected occurrence.

Camel. Unexpected news. Fortitude.

Candle. Revelation. Light on your path.

Cannon. News of a soldier.

Cap. There is a need for caution. *See **Hat**.*

Car. Good fortune. A change of surroundings. A trip.

Cart. A delay, but a business venture will be successful. *See **Wagon**.*

Castle. A wish fulfilled. Strong character. A rise to a position of authority.

Cat. False friends or a need for independence.

Cattle. Prosperity will be yours.

Chain. Marriage. Responsibilities.

Chair. A visitor. Take time to relax.

Cherries. Your love affair will be happy.

Chessmen. Beware of difficulties ahead.

Chicken. Ability. Industriousness. Cowardice. *See* ***Hen*** *or* ***Rooster.***

Child. Innocence. A new enterprise.

Chimney. Proceed with great caution in what you're about to do.

Church. Faith. Aspirations. A ceremony: wedding, funeral, etc. Unexpected money, perhaps a legacy.

Cigar. A new friend.

Circle. *See* ***Wheel.***

Broken. Unfinished business, a disappointment or a delay.

Closed. Good luck. Completion. You will bring your work to perfection.

Claw. Hidden enemy.

Clock. Hurry, don't hesitate. The sitter is thinking about the future. Look to surrounding symbols.

Clouds. A period of trouble.

Dots nearby. Trouble over money.

Clover. Good luck soon. Prosperity and happiness. You will forsake your present attachment for fresh young innocence. *At bottom of cup.* The luck will take time to arrive.

Clown. One who may seem foolish to you now will eventually prove his wisdom.

Club. It was a small wrong you committed, but make amends immediately. The leaves foretell you will be found out.

Coat. A parting.

Coffee pot. A pleasant gathering of friends.

Coin. Success in some business obligation. You will be able to pay your debts. *See* ***Money.***

Column. Support in your aspirations.

Comb. Release from small worries or obligations.

Comet. An event of unbelievable splendor will light up your life.

Compass. Choose a new direction. The one you are now following will lead nowhere.

Cork. Secrets you must keep to yourself.

Corkscrew. Trouble caused by curiosity.

Cow. You will soon have to make a choice between love and loyalty. Loyalty will win.

Crab. An enemy. Someone in your life whose astrological sun sign is Cancer.

Cradle. Newcomer to the family.

Crescent. Romance with an exotic stranger, under exotic circumstances, or in an exotic place.

Cross. You may soon experience an affliction. Or, you are merely coming to a crossroad or turning point in your life.

A wise decision means happiness greater than you have ever experienced.

Cross within a circle. The approaching turning point is surrounded by indecision. A lucky accident may guide you better than a deliberate choice.

Crown. Honor. Respect. Great abundance or great success. Your wish will come true.

Crutches. Help from a friend.

Cup. Happiness. Fulfillment. Success.

Wine glass/cup. Beware.

Water glass. Integrity.

Curtain. A secret has been kept.

Open curtain. If curtain is drawn back, the secret is not important.

D

Daffodil. Success. Great wealth. *See* ***Flower.***

Dagger. Danger. Impetuosity.

Daisy. Simplicity. Charm. Happiness in love. Easy acquisition of lovers. *See* ***Flower.***

Dancer. Exuberance.

Dashes. You are approaching a period of great excitement. Enjoy the thrills, but keep your head. A project is started but has a long way to go.

Deer. Arguments if you're not careful.

Desk. A letter concerning business.

Diamond. Wealth and luxury.

Dish. Domestic quarrels.

Dog. True friendship.

At bottom of cup. A friend may be in trouble.

Hang dog. A friend may suffer because you didn't keep your mouth shut.

Running dog. Good news and a happy meeting.

Donkey. Stubbornness. Patience. Pride stands in the way of happiness. *See **Jackass**.*

Door. An unusual and unexpected event. A new opportunity opens up.

Dot.

One dot. Emphasizes the symbol it is near.

Several. Money.

Dove. A message of love. A Quaker may influence your life. *See **Bird**.*

Dragon. A sudden change. A new beginning. An obstacle overcome that will change your life.

Drum. Time for a change. A trip concerning a new job. Scandals and quarrels are in the air.

Duck. Persistent efforts needed in matters of money. Fidelity.

Dustpan. Strange news about the personal life of a friend.

E

Eagle. Attainment of fame. Flights to new heights. *See **Bird**.*

Ear. Unexpected news. Pleasant news.

Earring. Beware misunderstandings that will cause trouble. Luxury to come. *See **Jewelry**.*

Easel. You will have an opportunity to learn new skills.
Eel. Distasteful duties to perform.
Egg. Good luck. Success. Perhaps news of a birth.
Eggcup. The danger you are in is passing away.
Elephant. Wisdom. Strength. Slow, but solid, success. Past help remembered. You can trust your friend.
Elongated S. A sign of beauty. *See* ***Letters.***

Sitter is a man. You will meet someone breathtakingly beautiful.

Sitter is a woman. By taking exceptionally good care of yourself and cultivating a cheerful and optimistic outlook on life, you will attain loveliness you never thought possible.

Engine. Hasty news. Energy. Let nothing slow you down.
Exclamation point. Excitement. A thrilling time ahead.
Eye. You will see your way clear. You will overcome difficulties. Take care, especially regarding business. Someone is watching you.
Eyeglasses. Caution needed.

F

Faces. A party or gathering. Friends.

Ugly face. A secret enemy.

Pretty face. Happiness. May represent someone known to sitter if a resemblance.

Fairy. An unusual symbol, seldom found. It means rare good fortune.

Fan. Flirtations. You will soon be the object of attention. A pleasant social event.

Fangs. Beware of trouble.

Feather. Fantastic good luck. Can mean instability and lack of concentration.

Fence. Limitations. Success near but you must overcome obstacles.

Fiddle. A musician. You could be procrastinating.

Fig. Fertility.

Finger. What does it point to? You have been singled out for something special.

Fire. Avoid overhasty reactions, especially anger.

Fireplace. The home. Warmth. Comfort.

Fish. One of the best signs. Good luck in everything.

With wings. Swift rewards.

Flag. Beware, danger ahead. A reward.

Flashlight. Vision. Insight. Something will be revealed.

Fleur-de-lis. France or something French.

Flower. Love and affection. *See* ***Daffodil, Daisy, Lily, Rose, Violet.***

In a basket. A bountiful supply of good things.

Fly. Small domestic problem.

Foot. You must make an important decision.

Fork. A decision. Two ways to go.

Fountain. Everlasting love, happiness, and success.

Fox. A deceitful friend.

Frog. Avoid self-importance. Changes bring advancement. *See* ***Toad.***

Fruit. Prosperity.

Frying pan. A project in the works. To be in a tight spot or "hot" situation.

G

Gallows. You will conquer your enemies.

Garland. Success and great honor.

Gate. Overcome obstacles and go onward. All is well.

Gift. Repayment. Surprise. You may win something or be given a gift.

Giraffe. Beware of committing a hasty or thoughtless act.

Girl. A child. Innocence. One's childhood.

Glove. A challenge. Justice will be done.

Gnome. A strange, but pleasant, experience.

Goat. Don't let someone upset you needlessly.

Gondola. Romance and love connected with water.

Goose. Unexpected visitors whom you will enjoy very much.

Grapes. Happiness.

Grass. Luxury and ease.

Grasshopper. Warning against improvidence. Caution against scattering your interests. News of a friend.

Greyhound. Good fortune in store.

Griffin. You are becoming eccentric. Beware of alienating your friends.

Gun. An avoidable argument.

H

Hammer. Ability to overcome obstacles.

Hand.

Clenched. A quarrel.

Making a victory sign. Success.

Outstretched. Help from a friend.

Handcuffs. Trouble. Restrictions.

Hare. A crisis will arise where only quickness of action and a decision will save you. *See* ***Rabbit.***

Harp. Romance. Harmony. A happy marriage.

Hat. New possibilities and probable honor. A present. A new project. *See* ***Cap, Sombrero.***

Hawk. Sudden danger. Jealousy. *See* ***Bird.***

Head. New opportunities.

Heart. Love and happiness. Follow your emotions but beware impulsiveness that may lead you into something you later regret.

Near a ring. Marriage.

Surrounded by dots. Love and money.

Hen. Domestic happiness. *See* ***Chicken.***

Hill. Small obstacles.

Hive. Activity. Future prosperity.

Hoe. Hard work.

Horse. A lover.

Approaching handle. A lover coming into your life.

Turned away from handle. A lover leaving.

Horseshoe. Good luck.

Hourglass. Time for a decision.

House. Domestic happiness. You are more fortunate than most people.

Human figure. Most likely represents the sitter. Possibly a friend or visitor. Study figure carefully. Note the appearance and activity. Look to surrounding symbols to identify the figure. *Alternate:* ***Person.***

Hummingbird. Guidance will come as a faint voice or suggestion, but listen well.

I

Initials. Represent people you know, or will know. *See* ***Letters.***

Inkwell. Letter containing good news.

Insect. Minor worries overcome.

Ivy. An old house will reveal secrets to you. True love.

J

Jackass. Stupidity. A foolish person or situation. *See* ***Donkey.***

Jester. Avoid frivolity at an inopportune time.

Jewelry. A gift. *See* ***Bracelet, Earring, Necklace.***

Jockey. Gambling. Love for a gambler could cause you great unhappiness.

Jug. Good health. Influence which will allow you to help another. An abundance of money.

K

Kettle. Comfortable old age.

Near handle. Domestic contentment.

At bottom of cup. Domestic strife.

Key. Doors will open for you. Freedom from something that has held you back. You will see and seize opportunities.

Crossed keys. Success in business and love.

Double key. A robbery.

King. A splendid sign of a powerful friend.

Kite. High ambitions. Something to lift the heart. Improvement of fortunes for you or a friend who means much to you.

Knife. Broken friendship. Separation. Illness.

L

Ladder. Advancement. Success. Progress, probably through hard work.

Ladle. Good things are coming your way.

Lamb. Peace.

Lamp. Celebrations. Success in money matters. Your study or reading will be interrupted by a stranger whose intrusion you will resent at first, but he or she will mean more to you as time goes on.

Leaf. A scattering of money, friends, or loved ones if you fail to pay attention to what is most important to you.

Clusters of leaves. Happiness and good fortune.

Laurel leaves. Valor. Victory. Control of a situation.

Pile of leaves. Clutter. Old habits. Outworn conditions or a large problem.

Rising up from cup. A rare sign. It is important that you pay attention to those who are dear to you.

Letter. News.

Letters. *See* ***Initials.***

Letter S. See ***Elongated S.***

Letter V. Sex appeal.

Letter X. Crossed paths. Look to surrounding leaves to see if a meeting goes to your advantage.

Letter Y. Choice of paths.

Lighthouse. Trouble threatens but will be averted.

Lily. A happy marriage, but pride could be your downfall if you don't take care. *See* ***Flower.***

Line(s). Importance depends on length and clarity of the line.

Parallel. You are going on a journey, perhaps spiritual. The goal is far from where you are now.

Serpentine. You are about to experience an infatuation.

Straight. Progress. A journey straight to the heart's desire.

Wavy. Could indicate a lack of direction. If long, signifies hardships.

Lion. Lust for power. Great ambition. The ability to win through strength. Could represent the astrological sun sign Leo. Take care you don't sacrifice someone you love to your ambition.

Loaf. Domestic happiness.

Lobster. Someone who seems unattractive at first will reveal a character of great beauty.

Lock. You are about to have an experience you will reveal to no one.

Log. Ambitions cut off.

M

Mailbox. A message.

Man. A visitor. If a child is expected, it will be a boy.

Arms outstretched. Visitor bearing gifts.

Distinct. The visitor is dark complexioned.

Indistinct. The visitor is fair.

Mask. Insincerity. Someone is trying to deceive you. Be aware that things are seldom what they seem. In the crisis you are about to face you will need to penetrate all pretenses and perceive the situation clearly.

Medal. You will soon be rewarded.

Mermaid. You will find temptation difficult, if not impossible, to resist.

Miter. You will be highly honored.

Money. *See* ***Coin***.

Cents sign. You are careful in the spending of small amounts, but you do not skimp on the big things that really count.

Dollar sign. Curb the materialist side of your nature, for it will surely bring you unhappiness.

Monkey. Scandal. Don't allow yourself to be caught in a situation that could appear compromising.

Monster. Terror.

Moon. Romance. A definite conclusion soon reached.

Mountains. High ambitions. Hard work. Success.

Mouse. Beware of thieves.

Mushroom. Sudden growth and expansion. An obstacle to be overcome.

N

Nail. Pain. Malice. Injustice. A new home. Relationship with an architect or carpenter.

Necklace. *See **Jewelry**.*

Broken. Something important still to be completed.

Unbroken. Success.

Needle. Trouble followed by joy. Something you've done will be talked about.

Net. Beware of a trap.

Number. Represents the time or date a predicted event will occur.

Nun. Your spiritual satisfaction must be pursued privately.

Nurse. Healing. Could indicate an illness. Take care.

Nut. A formal reception.

O

Oar. Safety from impending disaster, perhaps to do with water.

Octopus. Danger sign. Someone may be plotting your downfall. Beware of a complicated situation. You may be reaching out in too many directions.

Oriental figure (traditional). Asian culture. The Far East or Eastern thought.

Ostrich. Don't avoid what must be faced any longer.

Owl. A wise person. A night person. Something will happen at night. A mystery. Philosophy. Search for hidden things. Beware of a scandal that could involve you.

Oyster. Are you keeping pearls of great wisdom to yourself? If you aren't, maybe you should. A long engagement.

P

Package. A gift. *Alternate:* ***Parcel.***

Pail. Hard work in marriage, but much love.

Water in pail. An impending voyage over water is made interesting by flirtation with a fellow passenger.

Parachute. Escape from danger.

Parcel. A gift. *Alternate:* ***Package.***

Parrot. Gossip.

Peacock. Luxury and vanity.

Pear. Good fortune.

Pen/Pencil. Writing. News.

Person. Most likely represents the sitter. Possibly a friend or visitor. Study figure carefully. Note the appearance and activity. Look to surrounding symbols to identify the person. *Alternate:* ***Human figure.***

Pig. Mixture of good and bad luck.

Pigeon.

Flying. Important news.

Sitting. Improvement in business.

Pillar. Friends will help.

Pipe. Pipe-dreams. Indicates a man in the cup.

Peace pipe. An important conference. The outcome looks good.

Pitcher. Success through hard work.

Pod. Small start with increasing prosperity.

Pot. Service to society.

Prong. Necessity will help your cause.

Pump. A generous nature.

Puritan. Religiosity. Thrift. Simplicity. Boundaries.

Purse.

Closed. Riches.

Open. Take care or you will lose money.

Q

Queen. A woman with authority or who is of importance.

Question mark. Uncertainty. Outcome of plans doubtful. You may be at the mercy of another's will.

R

Rabbit. Timidity. *See **Hare.***

Railway. A long journey or pleasant experience will provide a welcome respite from your day-to-day problems.

Rat. Treachery and loss.

Rattle. Children.

Raven. Pessimism may stand in the way of success. Cultivate a cheerful attitude and all doors will open to you. *See **Bird.***

Razor. Sharp words cause trouble. Cultivate a more understanding outlook.

Ring. A wedding.

River. A fortunate sign. Your most treasured possession will endure forever.

Rocks. Obstacles to be overcome.

Rooster. You will have something to crow about if you stop wasting time and just do it. Freedom from financial worries. *See **Chicken**.*

Rose. Success in the arts. Friendship or good children. *See **Flower**.*

S

Sailor. Dreams of distant places.

Saucepan. Petty annoyances.

Saucer. Contented married life.

Saw. Strangers will interfere and cause trouble.

Scepter. Great fame from some achievement. A clash with authority. Look to the most dominating member of your family for help.

Scissors. Quarreling. Temporary separation.

Scythe. Danger.

Sea gull. A survivor. Gullibility. One who is easily taken advantage of.

Seesaw. Balance. Perspective.

Tipped. Moodiness. An unbalanced situation.

Shape.

Oblong. You are hiding something from someone. Someone hides something from you.

Oval. Beware! "Pride goeth before a fall."

Pentagon. Balance, mental and physical.

Square. Comfort and peace. Restrictions. There is a price

to pay for peace. Something of importance will happen to you on a street corner.

Triangle. If you are involved in a relationship triangle, remember that jealousy is fatal. Rely on your wits, not your emotions. *Alternate: **Tricorn.***

Pointing down. A disappointment.

Pointing up. Success.

Sheep. Good omen.

Shell. Good news.

Ship. Travel over water. Good fortune.

Shoes. A change that will point to success, probably new work. *See **Boot.***

Shovel. Digging oneself out of a problem. Hard work. Digging in. *See **Spade.***

Skates. Moving forward. Good times ahead. Momentum. A goal.

Skier. Pleasure. A swift road. A difficult climb.

Snail. Be patient. Be slow but sure. Your success will be all the more striking for taking so long to achieve.

Snake. Take care. Danger lurks concealed.

Sombrero. May represent Mexico or something of Mexican origin. *See **Hat.***

Spade. Hard work ahead. *See **Shovel.***

Spider. Determination and persistence. Intrigue. Unexpected money.

Spoon. Good fortune. Birth of an heir.

Squirrel. Happiness at home. Prosperity after hard times. Work.

Star. Good luck. Spiritual consolation.

Stork. Patience.

Stove. Home life. New projects emerging.

Suitcase. A journey. To straighten out or pack.

Sun. Great happiness. Growth.

Swallow. Swiftness of decision. *See* ***Bird.***

Swan. A smooth and contented life. A lover. Mystical insight. *See* ***Bird.***

T

Table. Festive gathering. Abundance of good things. Invitation. Business meeting.

Tangle. A mess or problem.

Teapot. A period of discussions and great social activity.

Telephone. Trouble because of forgetfulness.

Telephone pole. News of your love.

Telescope. An event taking place many miles away will affect your future life. Prepare for the future.

Tennis racket. An invitation. You are about to engage in a contest of skill or wit. Prepare yourself to win.

Tent. A vacation. A love nest for two.

Thimble. Changes at home.

Thistle. Happy, though never rich.

Tic-tac-toe sign. You will soon become intensely interested in games of chance. You are cautioned not to outstay a first run of good luck.

Toad. Beware of flattery. *See* ***Frog.***

Tomahawk. Gains by determination.

Torch. You will find yourself enthusiastically taking up a new interest.

Tortoise. Difficulties are eventually overcome. Over-sensitivity to criticism.

Tower. You will be offered a good opportunity. Don't let it slip by.

Tree. Good health and endurance.

Oak tree. Strength and endurance. Long life and happiness.

Palm tree. Happy and contented life. A large family.

Pine tree. All will be well.

Tricorn. A three-sided symbol. May indicate three interests, three jobs, three projects, etc. *See* ***Hat.***

Trident. Success in anything to do with the sea. A sign of spirituality.

T-square. Plans are being hatched that concern you intimately. See that they are to your advantage.

U

Umbrella. Shelter in a storm. Insignificant worry. Good luck through friendship.

Open. Shelter will be found.

Shut. Shelter denied.

Unicorn. A secret marriage. Chastity. Self-sacrifice. Transmutation. A solution to a problem.

Urn. Architecture. Classics. *See* ***Vase.***

V

Vase. Good deeds will bring future rewards. News of recovery from illness. Peace of mind. *See* ***Urn.***

Vegetable. Present unhappiness followed by content.

Violet. Love. A walk through the forest will lead to your desire. *See* ***Flower.***

Violin. Gaiety and much company. Individualism, perhaps egoism.

Volcano. Flaring passions. An explosion.

Vulture. Beware a thief. *See* ***Bird.***

W

Wagon. Slow journey. Heavy load. Wedding trip to foreign lands. *See* ***Cart.***

Walking stick. A visitor.

Wall. A lovers' tiff.

Watch. Secret admirers. An alert rival.

Wedding cake. A wedding.

Whale. Success in business. A sound defeat.

Wheel. Promotion. Fate about to take a hand in your plans. *See* ***Circle.***

Broken. Disappointment.

Complete. Fulfillment of desires.

Windmill. Enterprise. Success through hard work.

Wings. Messages.

Wolf. Greed. Jealousy. Someone will demand more from you than you should give.

Woman. Happy family. A girl child.
Worms. Scandal is near at hand.
Wreath. Happiness. Honor. Success.

Y

Yoke. Domination threatens. Beware of being too submissive.

Z

Zebra. Foreign country. Foreign friend or lover.

Glossary

Jung, Carl Gustav. A Swiss psychiatrist and psychologist who studied under Freud, but broke away to found his own school. His concept of the unconscious and use of dreams in analysis was a unique contribution to psychological thought.

Psychic Fair. A gathering of buyers and sellers of psychic wares, especially psychic readings.

Reader. A person who reads tea leaves for another.

Sitter. The person who receives the reading.

Symbol. Something that stands for something else.

Tasseography. The art of reading cups.

Bibliography

Chalmers, Irene. *Tea.* Potpourri Press, 1978.

Christiansen, Milane. *Tea.* Ventures International, 1972.

The Fortune Tellers. Black Watch, 1974.

Gettings, Fred. *Dreams and Omens.* Melvin Powers, 1975.

Hall, Manley P. *Dream Symbolism.* Philosophical Research Society, 1965.

Hunt, Cynthia. *Fun with Fortune Telling.* Reader Mail Inc., 1937.

Huxley, Gervas. *Talking of Tea.* John Wagner & Sons, 1956.

Jung, Carl G. *Man and His Symbols.* Dell Publishing Co., 1964.

McKinnie, Ian. *Fun in a Teacup.* Celestial Arts, 1974.

Schafer, Charles and Violet. *Teacraft.* Yerba Buena Press, 1975.

Showers, Paul. *Fortune Telling for Fun and Popularity.* New Home Library, 1942.

Woodward, Nancy Hyden. *Teas of the World.* Collier Books, 1980.

Zolar. *The Encyclopedia of Ancient and Forbidden Knowledge.* Nash Publications, 1970.

Index

H

I

J

L

M

O

P

R

S